My Community

J. Jean Robertson

ROURKE PUBLISHING

www.rourkepublishing.com

www.rourkepublishing.com

PHOTO CREDITS: Cover: © Yuri Arcurs; Title Page, Page 9: © Cathy Yeulet; Page 3: © asiseeit; Page 5: © Joshua Blake; Page 7: © William Britten; Page 11: © Gene Chutka; Page 13: © Steve Cole; Page 15: © Ron Chapple Studios, © Jason Lugo, © Monkey Business Images; Page 17: © Lisa F. Young; Page 19: © Frenk And Danielle Kaufmann; Page 21: © Sean Locke; Page 22: © Cathy Yeulet, © Frenk And Danielle Kaufmann, © Lisa F. Young; Page 23: © beth skwarecki, © Steve Cole, © Monkey Business Images

Edited by Meg Greve

Cover design by Renee Brady
Interior design by Tara Raymo

Library of Congress Cataloging-in-Publication Data

Robertson, J. Jean.
 My community / J. Jean Robertson.
   p. cm. -- (Little world social studies)
 Includes bibliographical references and index.
 ISBN 978-1-61590-326-9 (Hard Cover) (alk. paper)
 ISBN 978-1-61590-565-2 (Soft Cover)
 1. Communities--Juvenile literature. I. Title.
 HM756.R65 2011
 307--dc22
                                    2010009861

Rourke Publishing
Printed in the United States of America, North Mankato, Minnesota
033010
033010LP

www.rourkepublishing.com - rourke@rourkepublishing.com
Post Office Box 643328 Vero Beach, Florida 32964

My **community** includes all
the people who live and work
around me.

I deliver letters to all the people in my community. You can count on me to work in all types of weather.

Who am I?

A mail carrier.

I help people find what they are looking for in the library. I also check out books and DVDs to them.

Who am I?

A media specialist.

I go to school every day. I have many students in my classroom. I am not one of the students.

Who could I be?

The teacher.

We own stores and shops. People in our community come and buy things from us.

What are we called?

Merchants.

I am a doctor who takes care of the babies and children in my community.

What am I called?

A **pediatrician**.

We are **public servants**. When you call 911 in an emergency, we are ready to help you.

What are our special jobs?

An ambulance driver.

A firefighter.

A police officer.

When you stop by the ice cream store for a treat, I am waiting to take your order. I also take the money to pay for your treat.

Who am I?

A cashier.

My job is to give tours through the **museum**. I tell people about the things on display.

What am I called?

A **docent.**

My job is to help people learn to play games safely and be good sports.

What could I be?

A **docent**.

My job is to help people learn to play games safely and be good sports.

What could I be?

The coach.

21

Picture Glossary

 **community** (kum-MYOO-nuh-tee): A group of people who live or work near each other. Community may also mean people who have something in common.

 **docent** (DOH-sent): A person who is trained to give guided tours, usually through a museum or art gallery.

 **merchants** (MUR-chuhntss): People who sell items to make money. They might also be people who manage or own a store.

museum (myoo-ZEE-uhm): A place where interesting items are displayed. These items are often grouped by type such as art, science, or history.

pediatrician (pee-dee-uh-TRI-shuhn): A special doctor who takes care of children and babies.

public servants (PUHB-lik SUR-vuhntss): People who work for the government of a community. Public servants might be firefighters, teachers, or even mayors.

Index

Websites

www.hud.gov/kids/whatsjob.html

www.kids.nationalgeographic.com/Stories/PeoplePlaces/Firefighter

www.pbskids.org/rogers/buildANeighborhood.html

About the Author

J. Jean Robertson, also known as Bushka to her grandchildren and many other kids, loves to read, travel, and write books for children. After teaching for many years, she retired to San Antonio, Florida, where she lives with her husband.